The Empowered Parent

Thinking About your Child's Disability

Joseph E. Moldover, Psy.D.

Contents

A note about terminology

Parents

Throughout the book, I refer to "parents". This is for the sake of simplicity and not to diminish other caregivers – step-parents, grandparents, foster parents, and other guardians. The term "parents" reflects the parenting role and responsibilities, of a child's caregivers, regardless of family structure.

Learning and Developmental Disabilities

I often refer to "learning and developmental disabilities" and tend to use the terms interchangeably with "learning disorder" and "developmental disorder". I intend these to be very broad terms, referring to a range of diagnoses involving disruptions in the learning and/or developmental processes. Within this I would include: traditional academic learning disabilities, such as dyslexia; Nonverbal Learning Disorder; autism and autism spectrum disorders, including Asperger's Syndrome; ADD and ADHD; neurological disorders (such as epilepsy, cerebral palsy, and brain injury); and psychiatric disorders (such as depression, anxiety disorder, and bipolar disorder).

Introduction

This book is not intended to give you answers. It is not intended to explain the behavior of a child I have never met and does not presume to tell you what to think or do. The purpose of this book is to help you to think effectively about the challenges that you and your child are facing; to ask the right questions of the experts, theories, and treatments you will encounter; and to avoid the blind alleys where families can become trapped. In other words, it is about *how* to think, rather than about *what* to think. I hope that through reading it you will feel more empowered to think for yourself and to thoughtfully challenge experts like me when we sit down to talk with you about your child.

There are probably far too many books for parents of children with special needs already. In fact, if you are the parent of a child with a learning disability or a developmental disorder you are probably deluged with information. A search for books about "autism" on Amazon.com produces over 5500 results; a Google search for "dyslexia" gets you over 3 million hits, and a search for "ADHD" gets you over 13 million. The problem is that information does not automatically translate into understanding. Mixed in among the legitimate facts and theories are scores of myths and snake oil salesmen, mounds of outdated information, and plenty of material that may be valid for some families but not for yours.

Parents who come to me are often confused in some way by their children. They don't know why a child is behaving the way that he is; why she is not learning like her peers; or why he doesn't have friends. They want to understand, and to understand what to do, because their confusion is painful. Indeed, there a few things more painful than seeing your child struggle and fail, and not knowing how to help. Fortunately, the fields of clinical psychology and neuropsychology, neuroscience, and psychiatry increasingly offer insight into the nature of developmental and behavioral challenges. The nature of these problems, however, creates special challenges for those who wish to bring those insights to bear on the problems faced by individual families.

First, it is important to understand that this is a field that has lots in the way of knowledge and little in the way of "technology". In many fields it is not essential that the "consumer" have an understanding of the underlying science, because technology translates the knowledge of the expert into a form beneficial to the end user. I can fly as a passenger in an airplane without understanding a thing about aerodynamics, so long as the experts (the aeronautical engineers) have done a good job with the technology (the airplane). If you are ill you can benefit from technology (a drug) designed by a scientist, even if your knowledge of the disease and treatment ends with high school biology. For neuropsychology, however, there is no mediating technology. If you are a parent sitting with me in my consulting room, I may be able to "prescribe" a particular reading program, or a specialized school, or a behavioral technique but ultimately you, yourself, need to understand your child.

Second, the nature of these problems is such that they really cannot be managed by experts at a distance. If your child has diabetes you can put their care in the hands of a good endocrinologist. You will need to follow the doctor's orders closely, but in the end the doctor will be the "quarterback". Most parents of children with learning and developmental problems find that there is no such hand-off. An expert may be able to offer insight and advice, but ultimately you as the parent are the one who is shaping your child's development. To do this successfully you need to have a high level of understanding and to think critically about the information and advice you receive. It is my hope that this book will give you the tools to do so.

Diagnosis

Parents first become aware of learning or developmental differences at a range of ages. Some parents see something "different" in infancy when a baby seems unresponsive and uncommunicative. For another parent, the first sign of trouble may be when an 18-year-old who has always seemed endearingly disorganized comes home from college in the middle of their first semester because they can't handle the demands for independence. Many encounter the first warning signs somewhere in between: the five-year-old who can't sit still with the other kindergartners at story time; the seven-year-old struggling to learn to read; or the 13-year-old who is left behind socially in the maelstrom of middle school.

What all of these children have in common is that their development has, in some respect, diverged from that of peers. Or has it? Aren't there just some five-year-olds who are bursting with physical energy? Isn't it true that some babies are tentative and reticent? Does "failure" to assimilate to the social culture of middle school indicate that it is the *child* who has a problem? Is a child intense and mercurial or anxious and depressed? So here is your first question: *"is there a problem at all?"* This question will divide some couples and families for years. One parent may be convinced that there is a problem and accuse the other of being "in denial." The partner may insist that there is not a problem and suggest the other is "overreacting".

A Pragmatic View of Diagnosis

Let's first spend a few moments with this basic question: *"is there a problem?"* Should you, as a parent, start down this road of assessment and diagnosis for your child? If you are struggling with this question, I suggest that one useful view may be a very pragmatic one: *is the way that my child is thinking/learning/behaving <u>working</u> for him or her?*

This question is deceptively simple. There are times when things are obviously not working the right way. A child may clearly not be making developmental progress; this is a child who is simply not mastering the skills that they need to at their stage of development (for instance, not speaking as a toddler, not relating to other kids in pre-school, or not reading as an elementary school student). In other cases, a child is suffering emotionally and there is a need to find out why. And in still other cases, it is others who are doing the suffering…these are cases of children who are acting out and hurting those around them, sometimes physically but also verbally and emotionally. These are all kids who clearly need evaluation to determine what the underlying problem is.

But what about more subtle cases? The child who is not obviously in deep pain, is not egregiously acting out, and is not grossly failing to meet milestones…how do we decide what they need? In these cases, I think that it is very helpful to think about the concept of <u>efficiency</u>.

Imagine a machine that makes ketchup. You put tomatoes in one end and bottles of ketchup come out the other. You expect that, say, 10 tomatoes will make one bottle of ketchup. And then one day you observe that…wait a minute, you are pouring in dozens of tomatoes at one end, but only two or three bottles of ketchup are coming out the other!

I perceive many kids' processing problems as being like the faulty ketchup machine. These are kids who put in effort – academic effort, social effort, effort to control their own behavior and mood – and the payoff is meager. They are expending disproportionate effort for the results. They try hard in school, but their grades don't reflect it. They are kind and well-meaning socially, but don't click with any of the other kids. They strive to be "good", but their anger keeps getting the better of them. These kids, like the inefficient ketchup machine, are not "broken"…they are "working", they are manufacturing "ketchup"…but at great cost. And for many of them, the ultimate result will be exactly what it is for the inefficient machine – overheating and meltdown. When you see your child displaying this asymmetry between effort and outcome then they need the adults in their life to take a closer look and to connect with a professional to diagnose the problem.

Assessment: Who to see?

If you have decided to seek out professional help in determining whether there is a learning or developmental issue then there are a range of options for you. The first question you will face is: "where should I take my child?" Assessment of learning and developmental functioning is carried out in a range of ways by members of a wide variety of professions within both the health care and the educational systems.

Pediatricians and family doctors monitor a child's developmental milestones within the context of well-child visits. When development is disrupted dramatically they will often screen for an underlying medical cause and may refer to a medical specialist – such as a neurologist – for additional medical assessment. This type of screening may identify the rare major neurological anomaly, but it is important to understand that there are many neurologically-based processing problems which are not evident on medical evaluation. As dramatic and impressive as modern neuroimaging is, it is not yet used to diagnosis most neurodevelopmental disorders. A child with ADHD, or dyslexia, or Asperger's Syndrome will likely have a normal neurological examination and a normal MRI. Therefore a medical screening, whether by the primary care doctor or by a specialist, is what we would call "specific but not sensitive". This means that if something is found it should be taken very seriously...but the reverse is not necessarily true; the lack of a finding does not guarantee that all is well.

It is also important to recognize that the training for many, if not most, primary care physicians does not include substantial exposure to learning or developmental needs. Medical education, understandably, focuses on medical diagnosis and disorder. It is often the case, therefore, that more subtle developmental issues will not quickly be recognized by a child's primary care doctor. Moreover, from the primary care doctor's perspective, the patient with a true learning or developmental problem is a little bit like a needle in a haystack! These professionals see so many families and of these a very large proportion express some level of concern about their child's development. Are they talking on time? Walking on time? Is it normal for them to take awhile to read or to connect with other kids? The vast majority of the time the child is fine. Picking out the one case of true developmental atypicality from the pool of concerned parents is a monumental task for a pediatrician, regardless of their level of training. This is particularly true when there is a limited amount of time which medical systems and insurers commonly allot for well child visits.

So your child's primary care doctor is a good place to start, but it is often important to look further. Another venue for seeking help is your local school. Neurodevelopmental disorders span the border between medicine and education. Within the public school system there are generally special education professionals whose job it is to identify children with these challenges. School psychologists assess intellectual functioning (more on that later) and also often screen for emotional problems and various processing problems. Occupational therapists and physical therapists assess sensory and motor functioning. Speech pathologists look at speech and oral language. Special educators test academic skills. These professionals are immersed, day in and day out, in the school community and they often have a strong sense for children who are struggling. The opportunity to access these professionals in the public schools for assessment (and sometimes for treatment) represents an enormously positive and progressive attitude towards education. We, as a society, are saying that we are not going to let struggling children sink in a "survival of the fittest" atmosphere; rather, we are going to invest in identification of vulnerable children and support their progress.

While this sounds like an ideal place for answers, the system is not perfect. In my experience parents often voice several concerns with school-based evaluations:

- First, these evaluations tend to be descriptive, but not diagnostic. Generally school assessments are measurements to see whether a child has fallen behind in some way. They typically are limited in the degree to which they identify underlying causes of lack of progress and also in the degree to which they make prognoses about the future.

- Second, as noted above, the evaluations are often carried out by several different professionals working within their areas of expertise. The issue which this can create is one of integration. Sometimes schools are not able to put all of the pieces of the puzzle together into a cohesive picture of the child that can guide decision making.

- Finally, there is the touchy subject of money (you will find that this will come up again and again throughout this book). In theory, financial considerations are not supposed to play into school district's decision to assess, or their interpretation of assessment results. They are mandated by the federal government to provide a "free and appropriate public education" to every child, no matter how costly it may be for a child with a disability. In practice, however, this is a heavily underfunded mandate. Typically, the federal government and the states underfund their contributions to these programs. As such, individual cities and towns are faced with explosive costs – particularly in the modern environment, where parents are increasingly aware of developmental syndromes, and where (often expensive) treatments proliferate. The point is that, when the institution responsible for performing an assessment is going to have to pay a large part of the bill for any problems it finds, there is a built in conflict of interest.

There is also the option of having a private evaluation. Depending on the type of concern you have you may choose a professional with a specific focus. This includes speech-language pathologists, occupational therapists, and psychologists. There are also professionals such as myself, who are called neuropsychologists. Neuropsychology is a specialized field within clinical psychology which deals with neurologically-based processing issues. It began with the study of adults with different neurological problems – veterans with brain injuries, for instance. In more recent years, child neuropsychologists have also become interested in studying and helping children who learn and develop differently. The neuropsychological evaluation is a detailed process which often brings subtle learning issues to light. The knowledge that we now have about memory, organization, self-control, and a range of other areas is often very useful in helping parents and teachers to understand the problems and needs of children with learning and developmental issues.

In the spirit of full disclosure I should say that independent evaluation is the area in which I have built my career. In performing these evaluations I have the luxury of being able to make recommendations without financial considerations; I can simply think about what is best for the child. On the other hand, having an evaluation done privately presents its own challenges. Often, aspects of developmental evaluations are classified by insurance companies as educational in nature or otherwise as "not medically necessary," potentially leaving you with the bill. Moreover, financial incentives may run the other way. If you are being seen in a for-profit, entrepreneurial health care setting problems identified may lead to the provision of costly treatments by the same agency and there may be an incentive to over-pathologize in order to drum up business.

At the end of the day, when you are deciding where an evaluation should be done and by whom, I think that you need to focus on cost and experience. However, you must also consider the scope of their practice. Are they exclusively in pediatrics, or are children the minority of their practice? It's hard to overstate the value of experience in building a professional's judgment. You also must consider the person's familiarity with the system with which you want them to interact. For instance, if your primary concerns about your child pertain to reading and you want an evaluator to think about advising and consulting with the school then you may be frustrated going to a major medical center for the evaluation. The worlds of institutional health care and education are very different. For instance, I know many professionals who work in great hospitals who literally *can't* go to a patient's school to consult because there is no applicable medical billing code with which to bill for the time. Conversely, if your child has a neurological disorder and you hope to get help with issues like walking and vision, a medical center may be just the place. A community based practitioner may have more limited resources to offer for such a concern.

Don't be shy about quizzing a professional who you are considering for the job of evaluating your child. You also should feel comfortable going around to meet several different people before you settle on one. If you are not comfortable with the person who is lined up to do the evaluation you should look elsewhere. One great question to ask a prospective evaluator is: *"why do you do this sort of work?"* or *"what got you into this field?"* Some parents recently asked me this in an initial interview and I think that they really got to know about who I am in a way that most other parents don't. A professional's response to that question tells you not only about their background, but also about their professional commitment, their emotional connection to the work, and their personality – all factors that will help you know if they are a good match for your child, your family and your needs.

I mentioned in the introduction that it is critical that parents develop a strong understanding of their own child's profile and needs. As you have likely discovered, this is an ongoing process. So another important question to ask is: *"will the evaluator be available and responsive on an ongoing basis?"* If you go into a radiology clinic for an x-ray it is unlikely that you are going to need an ongoing dialogue with the doctor in the months and years to come. You will get your result and be on your way. Not so with developmental or neuropsychological assessment. As your child grows older, you may see behaviors or encounter learning challenges that you will want to bring back to the evaluator. You will wonder whether a particular issue is connected to the diagnosis that they gave you or whether it is something different? Is a new observation something you should be concerned about or does it seem to be as expected? Moreover, as you try different approaches to helping your child, you may want to go back to the evaluator to get some insight into whether the interventions are working. For all of these reasons, it is crucial that you work with someone who will be responsive to you in the long term. Are they readily reachable by phone? Do they welcome email from clients? How long does it take to get an appointment to consult with them in an urgent situation?

There is a very specific question which few parents ask when they take their child to an evaluator: *"how long does it take to get a written report of the evaluation results and recommendations?"* This may seem like a very mundane issue, but it's not. The written report is likely to be much more important to you than you realize at the outset. For instance, if you are hoping to share the results of the evaluation with your child's school and perhaps to amend their programming, it is almost certain that you will need the full report in order to initiate any action. Yet many evaluators get into the bad habit of falling behind in their writing, and as a result families have to wait for months – sometimes many months – until they get a written document. Imagine being told by a clinician that your child critically needs certain services, but that you need to wait to get their written recommendation for those services to be put in place. Now imagine that you wait three or four – or eleven or twelve – months, and no report is forthcoming. It's a position which families too often find themselves in and it hamstrings them as they go about trying to get their child's needs met. It is critical to understand a particular evaluator's turn-around time before you commit to working with them.

One key consideration that parents often don't think about is the financial structure of the system in which an evaluation is being performed...public school, private clinic, teaching hospital, etc. In every case, there are financial incentives in play. We don't like to think of our doctors and our schools as taking money into account (particularly when it comes to our children) but it is inescapable and therefore must be understood. Is there a bias to do less? To do more? To exaggerate problems? To minimize them? My point here is not that doctors and school administrators are dishonest or only out for their own gain. Few people go into education or child development to get rich (and any who do are quickly disappointed.) The vast majority of the professionals you encounter in these professions are good people who care deeply about kids. My point is that every single one of us operates within an economic structure and understanding that structure will help you to be a better consumer of the information that comes out of it.

I have to make one final comment regarding your decision. I think that the evaluator's professional and academic credentials are often overvalued. I've seen many people with impressive resumes and academic positions who are pretty poor as clinicians. Sometimes it is because they would rather be doing research then engaged in messy clinical work. Sometimes it is because their reputation is built around expertise in one particular condition and they see everything through that lens (for instance, an expert in ADHD who sees every struggling child as having that diagnosis.) Regardless, don't be "wowed" just because someone has lots of letters after their name, or is on staff at an impressive hospital or university.

Asking the right question of the evaluator

Oftentimes parents coming into my office have difficulty articulating *why* they are there. They may have been referred by a pediatrician, a teacher, or a friend. They have concerns about their child, but struggle to explain what they are hoping to gain through the process of the assessment. One useful rule of thumb is that you are unlikely to get the right answer if you don't ask the right question. To that end, I always try to help parents to express their questions about their child in a clear, concrete manner at the outset. Of course, there are endless questions that may be asked, but there are four basic categories:

1) Is there a problem? For many parents the fundamental question is whether a child's development or behavior falls within or outside of developmental expectations, and/or whether it conforms to the pattern of a particular clinical problem.

2) What is the problem? For other parents, there is really no question that what is happening is abnormal. The question is, why is it happening? What is the nature of the diagnosis?

3) What should we do about the problem? Once a diagnosis has been established there are usually a wide array of possible treatments, but parents are often unsure of how to proceed. In the next section I will talk more specifically about discerning which path is right for your child.

4) Is what we're doing working? For a child in treatment or receiving specialized services, the question may revolve around progress. Are symptoms dissipating or skills accumulating at a reasonable pace, given the child's developmental profile?

Taking the time before the assessment begins to carefully and specifically formulate your question can prevent great frustration at the end of the process.

What is done in an assessment?

I want to start with a distinction between "testing" and the broader concept of assessment. Tests are tools which we use to understand the way someone thinks, feels, or behaves. They are only one component of the assessment; a full assessment requires combining test data with everything that we know about a child's history and with observations of their behavior. For now, let's talk about the different kinds of tests.

Questionnaires

Parents hate filling out questionnaires. I know this because I ask them to do it all the time. These are generally checklists that ask you to rate how often a behavior or problem occurs, or how much of a problem something is for your child. I think that the key reason that people often feel anxious about filling these out is that they sense that their subjective perceptions and judgments are being calcified into numbers that will be interpreted as objective. This sense is absolutely right. Once we convert something into a number it somehow seems much more real. If you come into my office and tell me that your kid seems really anxious, then OK, that is your perception. If you fill out a questionnaire asking questions about anxiety and check off every symptom and I come back to you and say that your report of your child's worrying is at the 98th percentile...whoa, that suddenly seems so much more real and scientific! Of course, I have not really done anything new...I have not even given you an independent opinion about your child's anxiety. All I have done is converted your own report into a numeric form.

Questionnaires are useful as yardsticks. They allow us to compare your perceptions of your child's emotional state, or behaviors, or organizational skills, to those of other parents of same age children. Talk to any parent of an eight year old boy on the street, and they will tell you that their kid sometimes disobeys, seems inattentive, has tantrums, etc. What you want to know is, does your experience diverge from that baseline? This is the question that the questionnaire can help to answer. It is important to remember, however, that it does not tell you "why" only "how much". It is a yardstick, not an x-ray.

Performance Based Tests

This is any test for which we bring the child into the office and actually measure something that they do. A simple example would be a measure of reading speed; we can ask a child to read out loud and time them. Then, we can compare their time to data from a large sample of other children of the same age reading the same passage to see how they compare.

One obvious question is: why use performance based tests at all? Why bring a child into the office to test reading speed? Couldn't we just observe a class at school and note who seems to be the slowest reader? The answer is that most behaviors, such as a child's performance in a reading class, are "overdetermined." This means that, in any given situation, you are using multiple psychological functions. At this moment, you are reading this page. To do this successfully, you need to use your vision to see the letters, your language skills to understand the words, your working (short term) memory to integrate these words with those earlier in the chapter, and your long term memory to integrate this material with what you already think and know. You have to be able to sustain attention, even if there is something else going on wherever you are. You need to be in a calm enough emotional state to settle down and read. When you look at it this way, a "reading problem" is a very general term. There are so many different things that can go wrong and lead to reading difficulty. Any one of the links in the chain can be weak…each link must be assessed.

Here is another example: imagine that you go out to your car in the morning, and it won't start. If you want to do something about it, you have to understand why it won't turn over. So you need to look under the hood – you need to look at each potential culprit, one at a time, to see who isn't doing their job…is it the spark plugs? The battery? It's only after eliminating different possibilities that you will have some sense of what to do to make the car run. Performance based testing is like looking under the hood of the car. You look at each link in the chain, one at a time, to see which are contributing to the problem.

Take another example…a child in the middle school years is struggling with written composition. There are at least three things going on when a child sits down to write: 1) they need to use their language skills to formulate their thoughts; 2) they need to use their organizational skills (often referred to as a component of "executive functioning") to plan and organize their output; and 3) they need motor skills to produce legible handwriting.

So when a child has a problem with writing, how do we differentiate these components? Well, we would want to administer a motor test that has minimal organizational and linguistic demands, and a separate language test with minimal motor demands, and a visually-based test of organization that does not have language demands. By doing this again and again, over the course of a whole battery of tests, we can begin to pick up on the "thread" that runs through the child's difficulties – language, organization, motor skills, etc. What is the factor that pops up again and again, consistently acting as a troublemaker regardless of which other skills are paired with it in a task?

There are many different kinds of performance based tests:

- Tests of memory: visual memory, verbal memory, rote memorization, contextual learning, incidental learning, etc.
- Tests of visual-spatial perception and processing.
- Tests of all different aspects of language: verbal expression, language comprehension, articulation, etc.
- Tests of motor skills: hand-eye coordination, fine motor speed, etc.
- Tests of "executive functions": organization, attention, inhibition, and abstract thinking.
- Tests of emotional functioning: depression, anxiety, anger, aggressiveness – as well as broader tests of personality.
- Tests of academic skills.

Of all of the performance-based tests, the one which is best known and which has the most cultural and emotional baggage tied to it is the IQ test. This is a type of test which creates more anxiety and more misunderstanding than any other. For this reason, the topic of IQ testing deserves some special consideration here.

IQ Tests

There are few other areas of psychology which lead to more misperceptions and misunderstandings than IQ testing. Let me begin by offering my personal definition of what an IQ test measures: it measures a diverse group of skills considered to be pre-requisite for learning, particularly in a traditional classroom setting. I know that sounds a little abstract and nebulous, so I'm going to make an analogy to try to make it clearer.

Imagine that we wanted to be able to assess athletic ability in children (the test I'm going to develop here is purely imaginary, but it might help to shed some light on IQ testing). Let's say that we want to identify which kids were really ready to take off in sports, and also which ones should get remedial help. We would begin by realizing that "athleticism" is a pretty broad concept, and involves lots of different skills. We could make a list of the skills that go into being a good athlete: speed, endurance, eye-hand coordination, strength, etc. Next, we would create objective tests for each of those skills…maybe someone's time on the hundred yard dash for speed, the amount they are able to hoist in a deadlift for strength, etc. Once we had created this series of "subtests" we would take them on the road, measuring the performance of lots of different kids at different ages to see what is normal. Then, once we had that data (our "norms"), we would be ready to go to work. We could apply our series of tests to a particular child, assessing their performance on each one. We could assign a specific value to their performance on each subtest…speed at the 45th percentile, strength at the 75th percentile, etc. Finally, if we wanted to, we could average the child's performance on all of the subtests together into one big number…the Athleticism Quotient, or AQ. For the sake of simplicity, I might decide to use a scale wherein the average AQ is arbitrarily called 100, with lower scores representing poorer performance and higher scores better performance.

So what do you think of the AQ? Will it predict athleticism? I would think that it would do a reasonably good job of that. Kids who do the best on these tests will be the ones most likely to be the baseball and football stars of tomorrow. But there are a couple of finer points that should also be clear about the AQ:

- It is an <u>average</u>. Two kids may have the same AQ, but get there in totally different ways. For instance, one boy may have an AQ of 110 because his very high strength score more than balances out a weaker performance on a measure of speed. Another boy may also have an AQ of 110 but have a low score on the strength subtest which is obscured by very high scores on measures of eye-hand coordination and speed. Is this important? Are these two boys athletically the same, even with the same AQ? Of course not, and we need to understand the fine grained composition of their profile, not just the aggregate number.

- It only pertains to skills within its scope. A high AQ may indicate strong athletic potential, but does it tell you who is going to be a good accountant? Who has the best social skills? Who will be a really creative artist? Needless to say, it will not. It measures only what it measures; it is not the whole person.

- It is not immutable. What if a kid has a low AQ? Does that mean they are hopeless as an athlete? If I see a kid with an AQ of 85, my first question will be "what is dragging it down?" Perhaps they did particularly poorly on the strength subtest. What is the proper response? Should we just put the kid on the bench and tell them not to try, or should we develop a remedial program of strength training to make them as strong as their bodies will permit?

In the imagined example of AQ the above points may seem obvious, but they are frequently confusing as applied to IQ tests. IQ is the same as AQ, except that we are trying to measure preparedness for academic success rather than athletic success. Instead of subtests assessing speed and strength, we have subtests assessing pattern recognition and vocabulary knowledge. People make the above errors all the time…they view IQ as a holistic, universal quality, as indicating and predicting everything about a child, and as representing a core, immutable quantity. These misconceptions all too often lead us to sell a child short and to expect too little because a low score on a test "tells us" that there is little potential. This is a point which we will return to when we begin to think about treatments.

Judging the validity of your child's testing

As we start to think about what the IQ score means we begin to explore the issue of test validity. Is an IQ test valid? That question is asked all the time and there is not one simple answer. We need to ask: *"valid for what?"* Is it a valid predictor of athletic skill? No, absolutely not. Is it a valid predictor of preparedness for learning in a typical elementary school classroom? Maybe…but you need to ask a few more questions about validity when confronted with your child's test score. These questions apply not only to IQ testing, but to any performance based test.

- First, do we have a good sample? Remember, these tests are sampling behavior, not bodily tissue. If a child needs a blood test, we can hold him down while the nurse takes it from him, kicking and screaming. It will still be a good sample, whether the child likes it or not. The same is not true of behavior. To have a good sample of behavior, we need to have a child who is cooperative and engaged. A child who does not want to participate, who is not trying hard, who is tired or sick will give you bad data. In addition to the child's participation we need to consider the environment. On several occasions construction crews have decided to demolish structures outside of the office where I work. Clearly, I am not going to be able to get a good sample of thinking and behavior from a child who is distracted by a jackhammer outside of the window! This is an extreme example, but lesser versions happen all the time. In many hospitals the room dedicated to testing is small, windowless, and poorly ventilated. It may not lend itself to focused, sustained effort. So ask: *"what was my child's state when taking this test?" "What were the environmental circumstances? Is this a valid sample of their behavior?"*

- Second, what is the reference sample? As I described above, the process of testing involves comparing a child's performance to a normative group of peers. "Peers" is the sticky word here. Is it right to compare a child in the northwestern US to a child in the southeast, where the culture, language, and educational systems differ? Is it valid to compare a boy's performance on a math test to a girl's? What about race and ethnicity? Should we be comparing children to samples of other children from similar backgrounds, or to a more mixed sample? These sorts of questions have led to endless, heated, politically charged debates that stretch far beyond the scope of this book. The question for you is this: *"who is my child being compared to in generating these test scores?" "Does this seem to be a fair comparison group?"*

- Finally, we need to ask <u>what</u> precisely it is that is being tested. This may seem like an obvious one, but consider this example: I see many children in my practice who struggle with writing at home and in school, oftentimes to an extreme degree. When tested, however, they may generate average scores on a writing test. What is going on here? Well, the problem is that we are not being precise enough in stating what is being tested. "Writing" is too broad of a term. Some writing tests focus on the motor aspect of writing and the ability to control the pencil. Others focus on writing speed or on grammar and sentence structure. Others tap into a child's ability to plan and formulate a response to an open ended question. So a child who has writing difficulties as a result of disorganization may do great on a "writing test" focusing on spelling and sentence construction. The question that you need to ask is: *"what exactly was assessed here?" "What were the performance demands?"* And most critically*: "how do these performance demands mirror those of his day to day life?"* A child in middle school is being asked to produce large writing samples in response to open ended questions. There is a huge organizational demand. A writing test which only looks at grammar and spelling is not a valid or helpful writing test for this child.

Labeling and Diagnosis

I began this chapter by talking about situations in which parents are asking whether there is a problem. Various assessment techniques in various settings can be used to answer this question. Now, let's move on to situations in which we are not asking "whether" there is a problem, but rather "what" is the problem? In other words, we are trying to come up with the right diagnosis.

In most cases, diagnosis is <u>integrative</u>. There is not one single test or questionnaire for ADHD, or autism, or dyslexia. The diagnosis is the result of the synthesis of many different tests and the "configuration" which the data produces. I alluded to this above, when I wrote about the "thread" running through the body of data. Moreover the test scores are only one piece of the evaluation. The data has to be considered in combination with the child's history and the examiner's observations. Often, the numbers don't tell the whole story. One child may perform poorly on testing but have strong compensatory strategies that are clear when interacting with the child. Another child may have relatively normal test scores, but their "minor" challenges may have a major impact that is clear when you consider the full story of their history. This contributes to disagreements over diagnosis and helps demonstrate why it is so important to have a complete evaluation that integrates all the available information regarding your child.

It is also critical to understand that there are several very different kinds of diagnoses out there when it comes to learning and developmental disorders. I am going to call these "clinical" diagnoses and "relative" diagnoses. Let me explain how I define the two. Before I define these terms we need to remember that any problem that a child is having occurs within a particular environment...let's say, a 21st century mainstream American elementary school. It is extremely useful to ask yourself: *"is this problem specific to this environment, or would it manifest itself in any time and place?"*

Some of the children who come into my office are clearly displaying neurodevelopmental problems which would be disabling for them in any environment. They experience basic challenges in learning, in reasoning, in perceiving or remembering. These challenges make it extremely difficult for them to adapt. This is the case in the classroom, but it would equally well be the case in a dramatically different environment – say, for instance, if they were trying to learn how to work the land and to solve agricultural challenges on a farm 200 years ago. For these children, it makes sense to view the disability as being *absolute*; it is a clinical disability. Their brains are not fully carrying out the function they are intended to, in the same way that a diabetic's pancreas is not properly fulfilling its evolutionary function of producing insulin.

Contrast this scenario with a child whose problems in adaptation are very specific. Perhaps this is a child who is socially engaging and who seems bright when he has the chance to work with his hands or to perform on the sports field. In the 2nd grade classroom, however, he is having a horrible time making the connection between the spoken word and those little squiggles on the page. Moreover, he wants to move! Sitting behind a desk for hours each day is torture for him, and his teacher sees the resulting fidgetiness as disruptive to the class. For this child, the disability may be viewed as *relative*. There is a mismatch between the demands of the particular environment and this child's innate temperament and processing style. The environment demands physical stillness and sustained auditory attention; it demands close discernment of speech sounds and fluent connection of those sounds with visual symbols. Think about how idiosyncratic these demands are! If this child lived in another time and place, indeed in most other times and places, would his difficulty in meeting these demands be so problematic? Probably not; in fact, these demands would probably not be made at all. He might be an energetic and attentive farmer or an engaging and charismatic merchant. As a student in an early 21st century classroom, however, he is a square peg in a round hole.

So what should we think about the child with this sort of a *"relative"* disability? Should we ignore it or minimize it? No, the reality is that this child requires intensive intervention in order to succeed, as does the first child with the clinical disability. This child does live in a society in which certain demands are being made, and it will be devastating if he is unable to meet these demands. The point is that we need to be very careful about where we "locate" the disability. The disability is found in the interaction, the "fit", between this child and his environment. We want to be very clear about this, because if we are not it will be too easy to locate the disability as solely within the child and to send him (and you) the message that he is less capable than he really is.

Alphabet Soup

There is a well-known parable with which many of you are probably familiar. It is about six blind men who are asked to determine what an elephant looked like by feeling different parts of the elephant's body. The blind man who feels a leg says the elephant is like a pillar; the one who feels the tail says the elephant is like a rope; the one who feels the trunk says the elephant is like a tree branch; the one who feels the ear says the elephant is like a fan; the one who feels the belly says the elephant is like a wall; and the one who feels the tusk says the elephant is like a solid pipe. The lesson, of course is that all of them are right. They were all interpreting the elephant differently because each one touched a different part of the elephant.

I often think of this parable when certain diagnostic questions are raised. The unfortunate truth is that the field of diagnosis for children with learning and developmental disorders is poorly integrated. If you think about each disorder as an elephant, then the problem is that each one has many different blind men (i.e., professionals from different backgrounds) touching it and they are failing to talk to each other.

For instance, there is clearly a neurodevelopmental disorder characterized by social skills deficits, an inclination towards accumulation of verbal knowledge and verbal discourse, and often involving a limited range of interests and organizational difficulties. This entity has been studied from a behavioral perspective by professionals from a medical background for many years. Research began with Dr. Hans Asperger and the disorder resulting from this body of work still bears his name (Asperger's Syndrome). Elsewhere, psychologists interested in learning disabilities have identified a very similar group of children and labeled them as having Nonverbal Learning Disabilities. A group of British speech-language pathologists became interested in a similar phenomenon and labeled it Semantic-Pragmatic Language Disorder. Finally, occupational therapists interested in sensory processing viewed these children as presenting with a Sensory Integration Disorder.

What is going on here? Do we have four different diagnoses...or just one, viewed from four different perspectives by professionals who are unwilling or unable to come together and develop an integrated, comprehensive system of neurodevelopmental diagnosis? This is a tremendously complicated question, and it is certainly not reasonable to expect that you as a parent will work out the problems of inter-disciplinary collaboration as part of caring for your child. What you are faced with, however, is the need to sort out an alphabet soup. If your child is diagnosed with AS, NLD, SID, and S-PLD, what do you do? How do you think about the validity, not only of your child's testing, but of the resulting diagnoses?

What is a valid diagnosis?

Some diagnoses make sense, others don't. Just because a person or an organization proposes a label for a particular problem does not make it a useful or a valid concept. Let's think this through with a made up example of a diagnosis that would not be very useful or valid – Social Skills Disorder of Childhood (SSDC).

Say that I, as a psychologist, decide to "discover" and publicize SSDC. I could write a book about the "epidemic" of kids with poor social skills, and I could develop tests to reliably identify it – say, for instance, a parent questionnaire about your child's social behavior and a performance based test assessing their understanding and interpretation of social conventions and their ability to generate solutions to social problems. Now, imagine that your child came to see me for assessment and I gravely told you that he or she had SSDC. The question you will be facing is this: *is SSDC a valid diagnosis?*

My answer to the above question is "no", and I think that most of you will agree with me. SSDC just seems like something made up, doesn't it? (of course, it *is* something that I just made up, so that makes sense!) It is useful to ask precisely <u>what</u> is wrong with SSDC because I think that you will find that many of these same problems characterize more respectable diagnostic formulations which you may encounter. Pennington's definition of what makes for a valid diagnosis is a helpful guide in breaking this down.

First, SSDC will inevitably be comprised of a very heterogeneous group of kids. Put fifteen kids meeting criteria for this "diagnosis" in a room, and they will look very different from each other. Some will be bright, sweet, well-meaning kids who are good at a lot of non-social things (like computers) but don't seem to "get" other people. Others will be kids with entrenched behavioral problems who couldn't care less about social conventions. Others will be kids with severe neurological disorders whose difficulty assimilating to social situations is reflective of a general challenge in comprehension and adaptation.

Second, there is no clear causal pathway to SSDC. It is a location with many, many paths leading to it. In other words, being given this diagnosis does not really explain <u>why</u> your child has social skills problems. I don't only mean this in a "big picture" sense, such as the question of whether the environment or genetics have caused this disorder. We really don't know the cause of many of the disorders we see and in most cases the answer is a complex combination of both environment and genetics. Rather, I mean that even though we have a label we still don't know *why* the child is struggling. It's a common misconception that naming a problem explains it, when in fact it easily leads us into circular reasoning ("why does he have such poor social skills? Because he has SSDC. How do we know he has SSDC? His horrible social skills!") So what I mean is that we don't know why this <u>particular</u> child has these difficulties…is it because he is anxious about social situations? Because he doesn't pick up on nonverbal cues? Because he doesn't have the language skills to converse effectively? This imaginary diagnosis doesn't answer these questions…and neither do many of the "real" diagnoses you may encounter.

A diagnosis needs to give us some insight into the causes of the problem; if it does not, then we have the third problem with SSDC: the diagnosis does not help us to determine what will be an effective intervention. At the end of the day, the reason we pursue a diagnosis is not as a matter of academic interest, but because we want insight as to what will make the child's problems better. Now, it is fair to say that we do not always need to understand the ultimate cause of a clinical problem in order to treat it effectively. My doctor has no idea what, in my genes or my environment, caused me to develop Type 1 diabetes in my mid-30's. Nonetheless, he is able to help me to manage it effectively…not because he understands the ultimate cause of the disorder, but because he understands the nuts and bolts of where things are breaking down. If you don't have that, it is going to be very hard to put together an effective treatment. You need to ask: *"does this diagnosis tell me about the inner workings of my child's problem?"*

Should you share a diagnosis with your child?

In Part 2 of this book we will be talking about what you do once you have a diagnosis that you feel is valid. Now, however, you need to ask the above question, which is both common and exceedingly difficult. I have seen children who are absolutely liberated by the provision of a diagnosis. They have long felt that there is something "wrong" with them and have felt deeply and painfully alone. The affirmation that their problems are real and are known to science, that there are other people like them who have walked down the same path they are on, can be transformative. Indeed, for some children and adolescents the diagnosis is integrated into their identity in a positive way. Some adolescents and adults with Asperger's Syndrome, for instance, playfully refer to themselves as "Aspies" and create a positive, cohesive culture around their diagnosis.

I often comment to parents that, in the world of children, there tend not to be shades of gray around learning. Few children have backgrounds in neuropsychology or special education. For kids, there is "smart" and there is "stupid", and the child who struggles is apt to decide that he falls into the latter category. Even if you decide not to share diagnostic label with a child, it is often meaningful to talk with them about their own cognitive profile, to help them to see themselves through a more fine-grained (and forgiving) lens. Helping them to bring together two ideas that seemed to them to be mutually exclusive – for instance, "I am smart" and "I have a hard time with reading," - can be very therapeutic.

On the other hand, I have also seen children who are crushed by their diagnosis. These are often children who have entered into a depression as a result of chronic experiences of frustration and failure and who have deeply entrenched beliefs about themselves as defective and incapable. One notorious trait of the depressed individual, whether they have a disability or not, is that it is very difficult to break into and modify these self-deprecatory beliefs. Many parents (and therapists) have had the frustrating experience of finding that any evidence introduced which contradicts these beliefs is distorted and discredited. You may tell your child that Dr. Moldover can tell that he is bright even though the way he learns has made it hard for him to read, but a child with depression can often find a way *not* to believe this good news ("Moldover works for my parents, he *has to* tell them I'm smart.") Dislodging these beliefs is the arduous work of psychotherapy; we will talk more about depression and therapy in a later chapter.

This is also a time when it is important to think about your response to your child's disability. We will deal with this in more depth later in the book; what I want to note now, however, is that in conveying a diagnosis to your child it is going to be important for you to model a positive, accepting attitude towards the disability. It is common to struggle for a long time with the issues of guilt, anger, anxiety, and sadness that come with a diagnosis for your child. It's not fair (or realistic) to expect that you be completely at peace with the diagnosis before you present it to your child. If it's a very "hot" issue for you and causing you a high level of grief or frustration, it is probably not the right time to discuss it with your child. They are likely to sense your feelings and to infer that, whatever you may <u>say</u>, the diagnosis is a catastrophic piece of information.

In sum, like so many of the questions we are facing in this book, there is no pat answer. Sharing a diagnosis, particularly with an adolescent, is often helpful and meaningful if done in a sensitive way (and with an awareness that many of these terms have taken on derogatory connotations in youth culture; many kids, for instance, use the word "dyslexic" to mean "stupid.") If, however, you are embroiled in your own struggle around acceptance of the diagnosis, it is probably not the right time to share it with your child. Moreover, if your child has already entered too far into the process of constructing their fortress of depression, then it will likely take more than a heart-to-heart talk to break through. The diagnosis may well be co-opted by the depressive process, and a formal therapeutic intervention may be needed.

Wrapping up the Evaluation

Parents often ask me what they should expect at the end of an evaluation. I have pretty strong feelings about this, mainly because I have seen so many families go through evaluations and <u>not</u> get what they should. So here is my take on what you should reasonably expect when you walk out the door after the assessment is complete, whether it is something you are pursuing in a school, a hospital, or a private office.

- First, you need to have the <u>diagnosis</u>. When I say this, I mean "diagnosis" in a broad sense. There are certainly many kids who don't fit inside a neat "box" and whose profile is not summed up in a pithy label. Also, not all evaluators are licensed to diagnose. This mainly comes up in school-based evaluations, where an evaluator's scope of practice often does not allow them to officially give a clinical diagnosis such as ADHD or autism. Broadly, however, you need to be told what is going on under the hood of the car.

- Second, you need to find out what the recommended <u>interventions</u> are. There are an enormous number of therapeutic, medical, and educational interventions out there (more about them in the next chapter). Some are valid, some are snake oil. Even the good ones don't work for every kid. Following the diagnosis, you need to have a game plan for your child because realistically, you can only pursue a tiny fraction of the many strategies (some good, some bad) that are out there.

- And third, as you understand the diagnosis and prepare to take a course of action, you need to understand what the reasonable <u>expectations</u> are. An evaluator may not be able to tell you everything that you want to know about your child's future, but you should be able to take away some sense of an "aperture" of possibilities – the best that you can hope for and the risks that you need to worry about.

Ultimately, you should expect an explanation…an answer to the question that made you begin this process. This seems really obvious, but evaluators often don't volunteer to offer up a clear answer. Sometimes it's because they don't know, but often it's because it's hard to tell parents something hard, or to explain something complicated, or to take responsibility for advising a course of action that will be challenging. I clearly remember the way that my stomach used to tie into knots when I had to sit down to give parents a difficult diagnosis. Discomfort on the part of the clinician, however, should not be a barrier to you getting what you need out of the evaluation. When you feel that you are encountering vague answers you should feel empowered to press for specifics. If someone doesn't have an answer for you then that's fair, but it is better for them to say that then to dance around it...it only takes three words to say "I don't know".

Treatment

Diagnosis, the topic of the last chapter, is relevant only to the extent that it is going to inform treatment. No one wants to walk away from an evaluation with nothing more than a label. They want to know what to do and how to do it. They also want to know how to tell whether what they do is working. If you think that there are a plethora of confusing and poorly integrated diagnoses out there, take a look at the treatment field. The proliferation of all manner of educational, therapeutic and medical approaches to learning and developmental disorders is truly remarkable. As a parent, you want to provide your child with an intervention, but how do you choose?

In any profession there are going to be talented, ethical people and there are also going to be people who lack competence or are more interested in maximizing profits than in providing quality services. One of the challenging things about this particular field is that it often combines a desperate level of desire for improvement and progress with what are frequently vague goals that have far-off time horizons. In other words, parents are understandably willing to try almost anything and to incur enormous costs to help their children, but at the same time it can be difficult to precisely specify the goals of intervention. Moreover, gains are often measured over the course of years, making it difficult to determine progress from week to week and month to month (or bill to bill). These are conditions that create an ideal environment for charlatans to exploit parental fear and hope. Again and again I have seen families who can ill afford it invest thousands upon thousands of dollars in programs and therapies with no evident beneficial effect. Even worse, these courses of action often displace the interventions that *would* have a chance of working, squandering precious time during the most developmentally critical periods.

As has been the case up until this point, my goal here is not to tell you *what* to think. I am not going to try to catalog effective treatments, to endorse or discredit particular therapies or programs. After all, there are interventions that work in some circumstances but not in others, approaches that are right for some children but not their peers. There are treatments that work well when applied by an experienced practitioner but are useless in the hands of a novice. My aim is to continue to help you to think effectively and critically about interventions proposed for *your* child and to help you to clearly articulate your thoughts and questions.

Asking for Help

In the last chapter I commented that a clear expression of the *question* is critical at the outset of assessment. In a similar fashion, I believe that a clear expression of the *goal* is essential at the start of treatment. And again, this is easier said than done.

In putting together your goal you need to articulate two elements. First, you want to express the <u>target</u> you are moving toward. In a concrete sense, what are you trying to get, or to get rid of? Second, how are you going to hit the target? What tools will be used to get from point A to point B? Let's break those down one at a time.

> *"I want my child to STOP... (hitting, crying, being so hard on himself, being so hard on us...)"*

> *"I want my child to START (reading, working independently, socializing more with kids his own age...)"*

There are almost endless ways to complete these two sentences. In thinking through the right targets for a treatment, I suggest asking yourself three questions:

1) What is the most pressing need?
2) What is the most fundamental issue?
3) Is the target developmentally appropriate?

First, what is the most pressing need? The psychologist Abraham Maslow talked about a Hierarchy of Needs, running from the basic, fundamental needs for food and for safety through higher-level needs for friendship, for meaningful work, etc. We can apply a similar model in this case. If a child is behaving in a way that is harmful to himself or herself, then the goal of controlling their behavior will need to supersede other goals, such as the development of reading comprehension. If a child is emotionally unstable then it may be premature to talk about academic interventions that they will not be able to engage with. This much is fairly obvious. Complicating it is the second question: what is the most <u>fundamental issue</u>? In the example above it seems logical to focus on controlling unsafe behaviors before worrying about reading – but what if this is a child who is acting out due to frustration in school because they do not have the reading skills to access the curriculum? In this case aren't we just addressing a symptom, rather than the root cause, by focusing on "behavioral control"? Of course, this conundrum brings us back to the issue of assessment and the need to frame the referral question; in this case, we would ask "we know that this behavior is abnormal, but what is causing it?"

Perhaps this is just a way of saying "first things first", but with a caveat...before we can have an effective learner, we need a child who is emotionally and behaviorally stable and who is focused and on task. Just make sure that the reason they are unstable or unfocused in the first place does not have to do with lack of effectiveness as a learner! So the question that you need to think about and discuss here is: of all the things you hope for your child, of all the goals you want your child to move toward, and of all the things you want your child to outgrow and move away from – what is the first step? We may want to wind up in Boston, but if we are in Philadelphia we might need to first chart a course to Trenton. Trenton may be unexciting, it may not be where you want to wind up, but if you neglect the first leg of the trip because you are so focused on the ultimate destination you may never get there at all.

Next, think about the level of developmental appropriateness. Although it is less common now, psychologists used to reference a child's "mental age" (as opposed to their chronological age). While there are problems with this concept, it is true that skills develop hierarchically, that they are dependent on the integrity of the level below them. Does it make sense to target reading comprehension when a child can't decode words? Does it make sense to set a target for independent functioning in high school when the child does not yet have the social skills to navigate peer relationships effectively? As parents, there are certainly times when our children are ready for changes before we are…but there also may be times when what we truly want for our children, what we think is in their best interest, is something that they are not prepared for. You need to ask yourself the question: "is my child ready for what I want them to learn? Do they have the skills that they need to hit this target?" If the target is to eliminate a behavior, you need to ask the same fundamental question – do they have the skills to fulfill the request to stop? Think about a child who is having repeated meltdowns in response to parental requests; the obvious goal may be to eliminate meltdowns, yet if the child is dealing with an anxiety disorder we may conclude that they do not have the developmental competency in terms of emotional regulation to consistently comply with your requests. They are not developmentally ready to tackle your goal. Instead of formulating a target around good behavior you may want to work toward more mature emotional regulation by articulating something along the lines of: "when she is upset I want my daughter to tell me rather than immediately lashing out".

Just as we need to get to Trenton before we go on to Boston, we need to pour the foundation before we build the house. We may have wonderful ideas for the roof and the gables, but they won't do us any good without a solid foundation.

Making a Plan

Having a target is necessary, but not sufficient. I can decide that I want to run the Boston Marathon, but I need a way to get from here to there. Once we have a target we need to adopt a method and select the tools that we are going to employ. This may include educational approaches; psychotherapy; behavior therapy; medication; and/or computerized tools. Note that there is not a 1:1 relationship between target and method. A depressed person's beliefs about themselves may change in response to talk therapy, or in response to medication, or in response to a behavior therapy plan that emphasizes getting the person to exercise and socialize more. A child with ADHD may gain greater self-control through the use of medication, but perhaps also by going through an educational program that emphasizes self-awareness and appropriate outlets for energy.

This is a very common area of family conflict. I have seen many couples who agree on the issue of a target (they are on the same page that their son's behavior is disruptive and inappropriate), but they cannot agree on a method. One parent may wish to use medication to improve focus and reduce impulsivity, while the other may feel that this is fundamentally misguided, that it represents a "crutch", and that the child needs to face more consistent and significant consequences for his behavior so that he can learn to control himself and to act the right way.

Imagine that the two parents in the above example are coaches in the dugout during a baseball game. Their team is losing, 5-4, and it's the ninth inning. They are completely unified around the target (to score two runs and win the game), but they are divided on the issue of *what to do*…one wants to bunt and play "small ball", while the other wants to swing for the fences. In baseball, these kinds of moment-to-moment decisions are governed by an overarching game plan that the managers and the coaches develop based on their understanding of the team's strengths and weaknesses. The decision to bunt (or to swing) in the above example isn't random, it's (hopefully) based on a strategy that they have rationally worked out. Parents need the same thing. Once they have agreed on a target they need a strategy, a game plan, to get there and they need to develop one rationally.

So - what makes a good game plan? A behavior is not a disease, but for the moment let's use the terminology of medicine and call the target identified above the "symptom" in our intervention. Using this terminology, consider the following idea: *a symptom may usually be understood as a solution to a problem that makes sense within the context of the* <u>*skills*</u> *and* <u>*beliefs*</u> *that a child has at that moment.* To change it we can change the beliefs; build the skills; or alter the incentive structure so that the solution no longer makes sense in the cost/benefit analysis.

Let's talk about an example. Say that Emily is a girl in the 4th grade who is "acting out" in class. She is hitting and pushing other children, is defiant and rude with her teacher, and is not doing her work. So here we have a clear set of symptoms: aggression, defiance, noncompliance. Her parents identify these as the targets; they want to get rid of them. As adults, we feel that these symptoms don't make any sense. Why would Emily behave this way? It gets her into lots of trouble, costs her friendships, and makes her parents worried and angry.

There are, actually, a variety of different hypothetical scenarios in which Emily's behavior *does* make sense. The purpose of assessment, the topic of the prior section, is to determine which scenario is true so that we can choose the right target. I'll run through three of them, with the corresponding strategy that one might use.

- Emily's academic <u>skills</u> may be limited; perhaps she is a stealth dyslexic and cannot handle the literacy demands of the 4th grade. She has the <u>belief</u> that if people find this out they will think she is "stupid" and won't like her. Her behavior makes sense because she would rather be seen as a "tough, bad" kid than as a "stupid" kid. In this scenario, attacking her beliefs in therapy ("people are going to like you no matter what") or altering the incentive structure ("I'll give you $20 this weekend if you are good and do your work all week") are unlikely to really help. Emily needs to build her skill set (to learn to read) to help to eliminate her behavioral issues.

- Emily may have the <u>belief</u> that the only way to get respect is to be tougher than the other kids and that obeying the teacher means that she is weak. Perhaps she comes from an environment where friendliness is seen as vulnerability and peers or authority figures are overly aggressive. She may have been bullied. These beliefs, however, are maladaptive in the classroom and Emily would be a good candidate for counseling with an empathic therapist who can gain her trust and help her to modify these thoughts.

- Emily may be a child with an intense, independent, stimulation seeking temperament. If her teacher and her parents are overwhelmed then she may not consistently be punished for her actions. Her classroom and home environments may be somewhat disorganized. The excitement of instigating with peers may be much more compelling than the mundane work she is asked to do and her behavior may have the positive effect of getting her out of doing work. In other words, the cost-benefit analysis may work out so that these behaviors really work for her! In this case, a behavior plan to alter the contingencies or consequences may be what is called for. If she is expected to complete her work regardless of her behavior, and she is faced with consistently negative (but not physically punitive) consequences for her undesirable actions, then the calculus behind them may quickly change. Moreover, if she is supported in developing outlets for her energy that are more socially adaptive – skills in sports or the arts, for instance – then she may shift away from the problem behaviors because she can meet her needs for attention and excitement in a way that comes with fewer negative side effects.

We all have our temperamental inclinations. In my baseball example, there are some coaches who just love "small ball", who like to move runners around the bases a little bit at a time…and then there are coaches who want to go for the big home run that wins it all in one swing. Similarly, as parents we tend to favor particular strategies. There are parents who go to the incentive system no matter what. The incentive system does not need to be a conscious process or a formal system. It can be the laminated sheet with stickers on the fridge but it can also be less structured. It can be the parent who yells louder and louder and levies more and more draconian punishments, with the implicit reasoning that at some point the consequences – the "downside" – of the target behavior will tip the scale in the desired direction. At some point the kid will learn that it's just not worth it to stay out too late/skip homework/talk back/etc. At the same time, we may have a parent who is constantly bemoaning a child's "inability" to do their homework (or behave in church or share with other kids) making the blanket assumption that if the child is not doing what the parent wants then it must be because they aren't able to do so.

I mentioned earlier that choice of target is an excellent referral question in evaluation. Choice of strategy is another. For instance, a professional can help you to determine whether your child really can't do their 7th grade math homework. A professional can tell you whether your child really does have ADHD. A professional can tell you whether your daughter's interpersonal problems are rooted in an underlying lack of social understanding.

Oftentimes, however, the issue of strategy isn't so much a diagnostic issue (as in the above examples) as it is one of parenting style. Parenting style is often unconscious and rooted in the way that you yourself were raised. Some children can be flexible and respond to a variety of different parenting styles, but for many children with special needs this is not the case. Their needs are more specific and less flexible and as a result there is a greater demand on you as the parent to be aware of your own style. To the extent that a child struggles to adapt to you and your approach, you need to do more to adapt to their needs. And in order to do this you need to become aware of your own biases and beliefs about parenting.

In a larger sense, therefore, this is an area in which parents have to hammer some things out between themselves. The issue of strategy is rooted in some very basic beliefs that we have about human nature and about the world around us: are we born the way we are or are we shaped by our circumstances and environments? Are people basically "good", achieving some sort of self-realization and success as long as they are unobstructed, or are people basically pretty lazy, acting only when they have to? Is the world a basically friendly place where you can and should reach out for help if you need it, or is it a basically harsh environment where you need to achieve self-reliance to survive? I'm not going to weigh in with my own beliefs here. As a parent and as a psychologist I have my own feelings, of course, but as with so many of the other topics in this book I don't want to give you *my* answers – I want to set the stage for you to find your own. In having this discussion, however, I do want to point out several common points of dispute between parents.

Getting lost in "can't versus won't"

This is one of the toughest areas of debate. Parents can endlessly debate the question of whether a child is truly unable to do (or to stop doing) something, or whether there is an element of free will in the equation. Oftentimes the discussion might sound something like:

Parent A: "you need to go easier on him with his homework – he can't focus for long because of his ADD."

Parent B: "oh yeah? Where was his ADD when he was playing video games for four hours straight? He can focus when he wants to!"

In navigating these discussions it is helpful to get away from the binary, black and white distinction between "can't" and "won't". Usually, if there is a discussion, we are not talking about something that is a physical impossibility for a child. We are not talking about the question of whether a child with paraplegia can or can't walk. Rather, we are talking about *the level of independence and effectiveness that a child can show in bringing their mental resources to bear.* They may be tapping into their brainpower to focus on homework; to tolerate frustration in making a transition from a fun to a boring activity; or to organize themselves to get ready for an expedition. And when we talk about this, we are inevitably going to be talking about motivation.

Let's take an example. Imagine that I am told that I need to go for a run three mornings per week. Let's say that I am not a runner and that this is very difficult for me. I go very inconsistently. In contrast, my neighbor might be an experienced, competitive runner who religiously runs six days per week.

What would you conclude from this example? It would be incorrect to conclude that I *can't* run, wouldn't it? After all, there are a few mornings when I go out and do it. On the other hand, would it be an oversimplification to say that I just *won't* run, and that my neighbor clearly has greater willpower than I do? What I think this example should make clear is that there is a gradient running from easy tasks (running, for my neighbor) to more difficult tasks (running for me), and that as we move along that continuum we are going to see the task being completed less consistently and with greater demand for motivation. My neighbor may roll out of bed and run with little or no motivation, simply as a matter of habit. I, on the other hand, will require quite a bit of motivation…unless the difficulty of the task can be reduced for me. There will naturally be limits on what I can achieve; I may not have the potential to become a competitive runner. But if I get some coaching, and practice consistently, running will become easier and I will do it more consistently.

To think about this a little bit differently, take a look at the chart below:

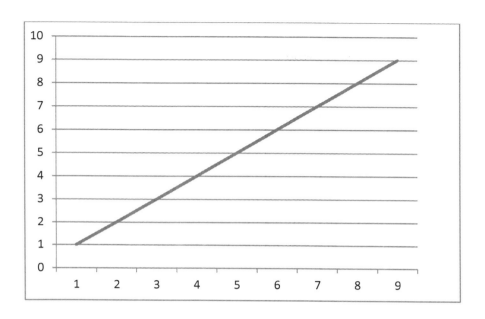

Imagine that the numbers running up the vertical side of the chart, to the left, represent the level of effort (and therefore, of motivation) required to complete a task. Imagine that the numbers running along the horizontal axis, at the bottom, represent the objective level of difficulty of the activity. The chart above depicts the usual situation, in which more effort is required with more difficulty.

So let's imagine that the task we are considering is that of catching a fly ball. The graph below might depict the level of effort required by a major league baseball player for this activity:

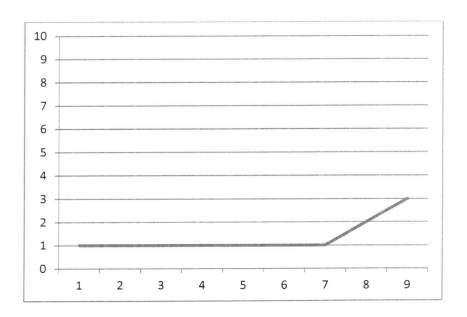

This person is so good at this activity that very little effort is required, even out to the right side of the graph. They can automatically, without thinking about it, track down pop flies that anyone else would find very difficult. It is only all the way out to the right, at the highest level of difficulty, that we see an upward spike in effort required for this player.

Now consider the chart below – it is a depiction of the same activity, but instead of a baseball player it is MY chart for catching a fly ball:

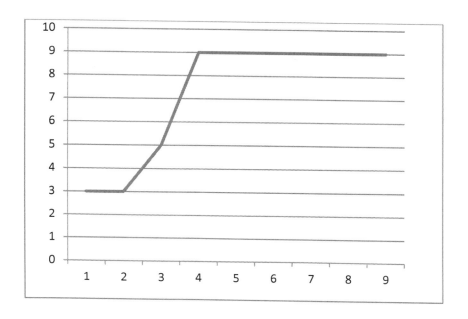

What does this show? I am not a very experienced baseball player! Even all the way over at the left side of the graph, with objectively easier pop flies (those hit close to me, for instance), I am going to have to invest lots of effort and concentration in being successful.

Now let's add one additional element: emotion. As we move up that left, vertical axis of effort we inevitable experience greater and greater stress. Conversely, at low levels we experience a lot of boredom. The question of *where* that happens is specific to each person and activity. In the above graph, I may be bored by pop flies at a difficulty level of "1", might be optimally challenged by pop flies between 2 and 5, and be stressed and frustrated if I keep getting hit balls that are in the 7-9 range. For the big league player, those numbers are obviously going to be different.

Let's go back to the discussion about your child. In all likelihood, we are not talking about a situation in which a child can NEVER focus attention, navigate a transition, or pull together organizationally. We are talking about a child who does this inconsistently and without a lot of independence, about a child whose graph for that skill looks more like mine than like the big leaguer's.

As you think and talk about your child's functioning, one question will be *what* is the "shape" of their graph for the skill or activity in question? The next question will be *where* on that vertical axis is their "cut-off" point? What is the level of difficulty at which they begin to display stress and frustration? In considering this you need to think about the "shape" of the graph – you might expect that a transition that would rate a "2" for you in terms of difficulty (turning off the TV and sitting down to write something) would also be a "2" for your child, but maybe it is an "8"? You will also need to think about your child's temperament – are they the type of kid who does well with "8's", or are they prone to anxiety and emotional reactivity, and best presented with activities in the "4-5 range?" The final consideration will be their history. Have they historically experienced success with "8's"? We may have two children for whom a reading assignment is an "8". One may have, in the past, tasted a lot of success with "8's" in other venues – pushing themselves hard in sports, for instance, or mastering a hard piece of music on the piano. This child may be able to tolerate being pushed with the reading. The second child may not have had those experiences. For instance, he or she may be a child with a learning disability who was been pushed too hard on academics in the past without sufficient supports in place and as a result learned that "8" is inevitably a precursor to failure.

The final question becomes *how*; which strategy will you use to make the behavior more consistent. Will you increase motivation by using carrots and sticks, incentives and punishments? To go back to my first example, I will definitely run more consistently if you offer me $500 for a week in which I go out three times. I will also run more consistently if you tell me that I have to work through the weekend if I don't get my running in for the week! It might also be a matter of adjusting the level of difficulty. I will also be likely to run more consistently if you give me some coaching to strengthen my legs and my lungs.

As you can see, we've found that the debate about whether a child can't or won't do (or not do) something (which is a dead end for many couples) can be turned into a more productive discussion about the right method to use.

Should you focus on changing the skill set or on changing the incentive structure? As I mention above, this is a complicated discussion and partly depends on aspects of your personal worldview. And again, I am going to refrain from imposing my own personal views on your thought process. I could tell you that I think that children succeed if they can, that attaining success and independence is the ultimate reward for any child, and that if they are not doing that it is not an issue of incentives but is an issue of inadequate skill base, or perhaps maladaptive beliefs (i.e., lacking the confidence to try something). Sounds reasonable, right? So lay off on the homework demands and call a tutor. But not so fast...I could also tell you that children respond to structure and that, like water running through stone, their development will take the path of least immediate resistance, and that it is our responsibility as parents to teach them the long-term value of doing what is not easy. Hmmm, that also sounds pretty good. Well – better sit your kid down with their books and let them know that nothing else is going to happen until they're done with their homework!

Allow me to digress for a moment. Years ago, when I was very early in my career, I overheard a casual conversation between two senior clinicians. One was telling the other about a friend who was wonderfully flexible and creative with her daughter. The child wanted to wear her bathing suit all the time, regardless of the season, and so this mom basically found all sorts of different ways to incorporate it into outfits, to keep is clean, etc. The point of the story was that this was a great mom, but the other clinician took it very differently. The second clinician said "wow, that's terrible. She's going to have a disaster on her hands when that kid becomes a teenager". Her interpretation was that the mom was being too permissive, was failing to set firm boundaries, and that this would come back to haunt her when the child wanted to do more than just wear her swimsuit all the time.

I was struck by the exchange because it seemed remarkable that two child psychologists could look at a simple anecdote so differently. It occurred to me that, were two pediatricians to be having lunch and one tell the other about a medical decision made by a friend ("she treated her daughter's pneumonia with herbal tea!") there would be a much higher likelihood of agreement. It also occurred to me that there was really no way of settling the disagreement. Of course, the child might grow into a teenager who is a holy terror – but she might not, and even if she did, how do we know that the parenting style caused it? Perhaps a third variable – the child's intense and independent temperament, for instance – led to both the swimsuit demand and to the later teenage behavior.

Although it was a trivial exchange, it has always stayed with me as an example of the pitfalls that we as professionals – and you as parents and caregivers – can run into when a decision needs to be made regarding parenting method. In many ways, these decisions reflect as much about us as they do about the children in question. Yes, there are times when I can offer a very clear cut answer. Using rewards and punishments to get a severely dyslexic child to read will not work well, for instance. More often, however, we find ourselves somewhere intermediate on the gradient of the effort curve, stuck between "can't" and "won't", struggling to balance firm expectations with a helping hand.

My advice for this discussion is twofold. First, understand exactly where your child is on that "curve". Know how hard reading is, or how hard it is to inhibit impulses, or how intense the anxiety is for your child. Second, talk about how high your child is ready to go on that vertical "effort" axis. Remember that the higher you go, the higher the stress. Given your child's personal history, their temperament, and their baseline level of stress, how hard can you push them? Finally, acknowledge the subjectivity of the judgment. If your partner is advocating a different approach, appreciate that it is an opinion that may say as much about their own background and view of the world as it does about your child.

Getting lost in the origin of a behavior

This is another pitfall that I want to spend a few moments addressing. I think that many parents get stuck in an argument about *where* a behavior or a deficit comes from, and this disagreement prevents them from doing anything about it.

First, it is important to acknowledge that psychologists don't fully understand the origins of many learning and developmental problems. If you start asking around about the cause of reading disorder, or depression, or autism you are going to hear a lot of competing theories, do a lot of reading, and wind up with either a headache or a PhD (possibly both). Luckily, it's usually not necessary to completely elucidate the original causes of these problems in order to do something effective about them. This is not to say that understanding causes don't matter, but it is to say that those causes are oftentimes divorced from the ongoing perpetuation of the problem.

Take an example: exercise. I might start exercising because I want to lose weight or because I've been scared by a warning from my doctor. So I make myself go running, or go to the gym, and pretty soon I'm hooked – I'm going four or five times a week, I've lost that weight, and my doctor considers me a success story. What keeps me going? Do I still drag myself off of the couch thinking about my worry over the medical warning I received last year? Probably not; I probably go because of the social relationships I've made at the gym, or the fact that being "a runner" has become part of my identity and I have cool shoes, or because I've gotten hooked on the endorphins. Again, the factors that *keep* it going are not the same as the factors that *got* it going.

The psychologist Gordon Allport called this the "Functional Autonomy of Motives" and it is one of those endlessly useful concepts. It means that the factors that lead to a behavior (or a behavioral problem) are not necessarily the same factors that keep it going. So many parents become lost in arguments over whether a behavior is due to genetics, or what the child has learned from TV, or bonking their head when they were younger, or whatever. Oftentimes these discussions are stressful, guilt- and anxiety-inducing, and can't ever really be resolved. More importantly, they may have nothing to do with the dynamics that keep the problem going. A child's problem may be genetic in origin, but it may be perpetuated by the nature of their educational environment. A problem may have originated in a psychologically traumatic experience, but it may be perpetuated by patterns of avoidant behavior and atypical neurotransmitter action in the brain. This is not to say that you shouldn't think about the cause of the problem – only that it is usually more productive to look at present causes rather than original causes, because they might not be the same.

Getting lost in the biology of a behavior

The years 1990-2000 were designated The Decade of the Brain by President George H.W. Bush. This recognized, and supported, the explosion of research into the neurobiology of behavior. This body of research has been a great thing for a generation of scientists, clinicians, and patients and it offers promise for new and more effective treatments for many disorders. It has also filtered into the common language, with many of us casually referring to "left brain vs. right brain thinking" or to our "frontal lobes" (or lack thereof).

One negative flip side to this revolution, however, is the potential helplessness that we can feel when told that something is brain-based.

To a large extent, this thinking error is based in a cultural thinking problem with deep roots in Western civilization. For centuries philosophy and science entertained the concept of the "mind-brain dualism", the idea that mind and brain are different entities with a mysterious connection. The relationship between mind and brain remains a fascinating topic, with many books available in the field of Philosophy of Mind. The question of whether the mind is identical to the brain is complicated. Few thinkers believe that "mind" refers to an ethereal substance entirely separate from the brain. At the same time, it can be difficult to accept that when we talk about mental concepts such as love, courage, or sense of identity we are simply referring to patterns of electrochemical activity in a few pounds of gelatinous substance suspended between our ears. Resolving this issue certainly goes beyond both the scope of this book and my own capabilities. My concern here is to address the problems that come up when mind/brain dualism leads parents to feel that there is nothing that they can do for a suffering child.

Parents will often ask a question or make a statement along the lines of: "isn't my child just hard-wired this way?" or "if this is the way their brain works then I feel like there's nothing we can do to change it". Remember, however, that to a certain extent ALL mental phenomena can be characterized in neurological terms. As you sit and read this I can describe the process in terms of activity in your optic tract, your occipital cortex, your temporal lobe, etc. Does this negate the process of reading, make it so that you are not really "reading" but rather doing something else? Obviously not, it is just another language for describing what can also be described behaviorally ("I am sitting and looking through this book") or psychologically ("I am decoding these words, thinking about these ideas and integrating this material with what I already know"). Remember also that the fact that a problem may be understood biologically does not make it impervious to behavioral or psychological intervention. My diabetes, a classic physiological problem, is very responsive to behavioral interventions around my diet. A child with OCD, widely recognized now as a neuropsychiatric problem with genetic roots, often responds quite well to certain forms of talk therapy (I once heard a psychiatrist describe his therapeutic approach as the same as that of a clinician who was prescribing a drug, except that he was "going in through the ears instead of through the mouth").

There is no question that the physiology is important. With respect to my diabetes example, the discovery of the physiological deficit underlying the disorder led to the development of the drug that keeps me alive so that the nutritional approaches can work. What's important is that the brain-talk should never be a conversation stopper; it should not lead to a sense of hopelessness or inevitability about a child's problem; and it should not lead to the dismissal of behavioral, educational or psychological treatments.

Who to see (and whether to trust them)

Parents often wonder exactly who they should go to for help. This is often a difficult decision, given that it is very difficult to assess the quality of a professional's work in such a private enterprise. If I am looking for a new mechanic there are probably a lot of people in my neighborhood who can tell me about the good (or bad) work that different garages around town have done, how much they charge, etc. Given that a child is so much different from a car it is much harder to track down this kind of information about counselors!

I think that one of the most important variables, after basic competency and experience levels are met, really has to do with personal fit. There is not much evidence, for instance, that psychotherapists with doctoral degrees are consistently more effective than those with masters or that counselors with one type of graduate training do better than those with another. Certainly, experience is important and you want someone who is knowledgeable about your child's situation. Frequently I have seen mental health professionals who are not familiar with Asperger's Syndrome misinterpret the idiosyncratic thought and behavioral patterns of children with that diagnosis. On the other hand the more junior and less experienced clinician may be more enthusiastic and energetic in engaging with your child than someone who is "burned out", so you shouldn't necessarily insist on the most seasoned professional! Your connection and comfort should be of the greatest importance.

The research suggests that the most important variable in therapy has to do with the quality of the therapeutic alliance, and I think that this is an important principle to apply to intervention in general. By "therapeutic alliance" I am referring to a particular quality of the relationship between your family and the clinician. It is a quality of trust and open-ness, and a sense that they are invested in your and your child's well-being. It is a sense of "we-ness", of being engaged in the struggle toward your goals together, and a feeling of being in the same boat. This is a unique feature of the relationship in mental or behavioral health. If you are hiring a plumber, a lawyer, or a cardiologist you are likely to be primarily interested in someone's technical expertise. It's best if you like the person, and there needs to be a basic level of trust, but, at the end of the day, it is a relationship based on their expertise to provide a technical service. Not entirely so with a mental health professional. Yes, technical expertise is important. You want someone who knows how to accurately diagnose, or to set up a behavior plan, or to engage a child with autism. You are also, however, looking for a particular relationship. And, just like when you are looking for a relationship on the dating scene, this is not likely to happen immediately or easily. You need to see lots of people, to meet with different possible matches, and to listen to your instincts as to whether this is someone you can like and trust. Interview different therapists. Elicit different recommendations from psychiatrists. Ask a few behaviorists how they would approach a plan for your child. Ask around and meet with possible clinicians until you are happy.

During these conversations you will need to think critically about each clinician's claims. This may be a claim regarding what their treatment can do for your child, or it might be an interpretation of what they have learned or what has been gained through treatment. An example of the former: "my reading program will move your child ahead by three grade levels in one month". An example of the latter: "through therapy, I have discovered that your child's behavior symptoms are due to insecure parental attachment". There are three questions you should be asking about these claims:

1) Is it specific?
2) Is it verifiable (able to be proven right or wrong)?
3) Is it proprietary (owned by, or specifically profiting, the person recommending it)?

First, specificity. A good rule of thumb is that a claim is more credible the more specific it is. Let's say that I want to offer you "Therapy Z". I might claim that "Therapy Z is effective for dyslexia, ADHD, dyspraxia, and autism spectrum disorders. It has the potential to improve your child's social, emotional, and academic functioning by stimulating their cerebral cortex. Through a program of exercises, it will become easier for your child to learn and to develop new skills!" This claim is adapted, with very minor modification, from the real world. It sounds awfully good, but is also very broad. Think about the range of diagnoses it is purporting to treat and the range of developmental domains (social, emotional, academic) it is supposed to impact. Think also about the vagueness of the claim to help "learning" and "skills".

Now contrast that with the following: "my reading therapy Q targets basic language skills, including phonological awareness and rapid naming, in order to improve word decoding and reading fluency". I am being very clear about what my treatment will help, and it is a very specific set of skills – word decoding and reading fluency. I am not claiming that it is also going to spread out and help your child's social skills or boost his IQ. Although I might claim that I can help kids with a variety of diagnoses to learn to read, I am not trying to simultaneously bill it as an approach to social issues in autism and impulsivity in ADHD. This is what I mean by specificity in a claim…and clearly, the more specific, the better.

Now let's move on to the second issue, verifiability. This is the issue of whether a claim can, from a practical point of view, be proven right or wrong. If not, I as a clinician am writing myself a blank check to do and say whatever I want, knowing that I can never really be held to account. Here is a nicely verifiable claim: "my reading program Q will improve your child's reading comprehension by at least one grade level by the end of the summer". And here is one that is less so: "my fabulous Therapy Z will reconfigure the synapses in your child's brain, improving the efficiency of cortical functioning". The second one sounds a lot cooler, doesn't it? It is also, for all intents and purposes, entirely unverifiable. Although words like "synapses" sound not only scientific but specific, the claim is actually very general and vague. When a claim lacks specificity, it will usually also be lacking in verifiability.

The issue of verifiability also pertains to a "big picture" question about the intervention. Let's say you have gone through the assessment process and you have received a diagnosis. You have identified goals and a method to reach those goals. You have found an interventionist to work with and have embarked on a plan. Now the question is: how do you know it is working? On the surface this seems like a deceptively simple question. If a child stops having tantrums, or starts reading, or seems happier, then it's fair to say it's working, isn't it? Perhaps, but all too often the goal of the intervention is framed in a vague, open-ended, non-empirical manner. I have no problem with working toward psychological maturity self-actualization, or greater insight. These are very worthy goals for anyone. The issue arises when these are the only claims offered to you, as the parent. How will you know if the treatment is working? How will you know it's not, and that you need to try something different? How will you know that it has and that it's OK to stop? In addition to the "philosophy" of the intervention (i.e., development of developmental maturity and psychological insight) it is also fair for you to ask for verifiable claims about what the treatment may do. This is not the same as a "guarantee", but it is a concrete, mutually agreed upon metric and timeframe to let both you and the clinician know that the treatment is – or is not – working.

A claim may lack verifiability because it is vague, but more subtly it may lack verifiability because it is impossible to establish the correct flow of causation. Let me give you an example of the latter. Let's say that we have a child with long-standing developmental issues, and a doctor interprets his late onset of puberty as an expression of his desire to stay a little boy and avoid facing the overwhelming demands of the real world. It sounds plausible, even somewhat poetic. It is also fairly specific. Buried in it, however, is an assumption about what is causing what. The assumption is that the psychological need is causing the physical symptom, that A leads to B. It *could* be as the doctor claims, but let me offer an alternate view. Perhaps this child's psychological and physical immaturity are both the result of some other third factor, such as a genetic predisposition to developmental delay. In this case, C causes A and C causes B. We don't know, and unless we somehow discover "C" (for instance, through a genetic test), we can't know.

Now let's talk about the last question, whether my claim pertains to something proprietary. In the earlier section on assessment I referred to the need to appreciate who benefits financially from diagnostic conclusions, and it is even more important to think about who gains from the employment of a treatment. This may sound cynical, but it is true. In general, one is more likely to recommend an intervention if one stands to gain from it. There is something to be said for the old model of separating the doctor and the pharmacy – your doctor makes the diagnosis of hypertension and prescribes a drug, but he or she is not the one to sell it to you. You have confidence that it's an objective recommendation, that the doctor is recommending that drug because it is the best one for your condition. Wouldn't you feel less confident if Dr. Smith tried to sell you, right there in his office, on "Dr. S's Miracle Hypertension Pills"? Don't be afraid to ask about this. If you are being referred or recommended for a treatment provided by the diagnostician, or in the diagnostician's clinic, it may very well be because he or she thinks that it is the best course of action. Don't let yourself be steered, however. Always ask for a second referral to a provider of the service not affiliated with the referring clinician (in most cases this should really be spontaneously offered, without your having to ask). You may not choose to use this and may stick with the first offering – but if you are told that "there is no one else", a red flag should go up.

As I've said before, I don't want to characterize every professional you meet as primarily chasing money or defending budgets. Most people, in both the private and the public sectors, are interested in helping kids. I don't think that financing is everything, but funding and reimbursement patterns do shape educational and health care, sometimes in ways that even the participants in the system aren't fully aware of.

Conclusion

Sometimes when we do something important the magnitude of it is only evident in retrospect – going out on a date with the person who turns out to be our future spouse; going on the 150th job interview; driving by the house with the "for sale" sign. When we're parenting, however, we're doing one of the most important things we're ever going to do, and we know it as we're doing it. This can be great when things are going well and terrifying when they are not.

When we're scared and confused there is a natural tendency to look for concrete answers from an authority and there's nothing wrong with that. There is a fine line, however, between this and blindly signing on with a guru, or an organization, or a movement, or subscribing to a theory or treatment wholesale. Psychologists have often observed that in times of societal crisis people are susceptible to demagogues…and the same is true at the "micro" level of personal crisis. Every day in my office I see parents and families struggling with their own crises. There is little that is more anxiety provoking than seeing your child flounder, and the repercussions can destabilize entire families. I see people dealing with these crises in ways that are inspirational, and I also see people being taken in by charlatans or frozen by the sheer cacophony of opinions and offerings around them.

It's also worth acknowledging that these are difficult times for families. Fewer of us live close to parents, uncles, and aunts. Fewer of us have a community doctor who has taken care of multiple generations of our family, and we often don't have personal relationships with the school teachers and the principal. We lack trustworthy voices in our day-to-day lives, people who see us with our children regularly and can speak to us from experience. Moreover, many of the issues discussed here were little known – or not known at all – in previous generations. A very short time ago concepts of learning disability or autism spectrum disorder were very different than they are today, and so even if we do have an experienced voice in our lives they may not be able to draw on great knowledge of the specific problems that we are facing. Finally, most families struggle to make ends meet financially. Fewer of us have the time or the financial resources to pour into these complex problems. When two parents have to work to pay the mortgage and put food on the table it becomes very difficult to invest the time and effort necessary to grasp and address many learning and developmental issues. Beyond that, these problems often fall into the space between the educational and the health systems, leaving families responsible for the high costs of assessment and treatment.

Throughout this book I've refrained from offering my advice, but I will wrap up with a few general thoughts. Raising kids is hard. Raising kids with special needs is really, really hard. Raising kids with special needs in an environment in which you are receiving multiple, conflicting pieces of advice and in which your emotional, financial, and physical resources are being stretched to the limit often feels impossible. If it weren't one of the most important things you're ever going to do I would tell you to give up. But since you can't do that, and since I'm not telling you what to think or to do, I will tell you some things NOT to do:

<u>Don't</u> be intimidated by doctors, special education professionals, and others with strong opinions and with authority. Listen to us, but don't give up your right to think independently.

<u>Don't</u> lock horns with your partner in an endless debate about the root causes of your child's difficulties or about the level of control that they have over their problems. Go ahead and have an open discussion; put your thoughts and feelings about the situation on the table. It's going to be a really personal talk because it taps into your basic beliefs about the way that YOU were raised and your hopes for your child's future. You may need to check in with someone who can help to guide the discussion, like a marriage counselor. But don't do down a rabbit hole with questions that can never be answered. At some point, you need to come out of this discussion and get on the same page with goals and methods.

<u>Don't</u> be afraid to reach out for help. Finding yourself confused by, even overwhelmed by your child can feel not only devastating but also isolating. Chances are, however, that there are other parents

nearby who have been through very similar experiences, or who are going through it now. These people can often empathize with what you are going through and offer practical advice. Parents often organize at the local level in special education support groups, or at the regional or national levels in organizations centering on a particular diagnosis. Although reaching out can be intimidating and difficult, it beats being alone with these issues.

Finally, <u>don't</u> give up. As I said above, quitting really isn't an option. You are going to be wrong sometimes. Part of thinking for yourself, of being empowered, is owning your errors. You need to accept that you are engaged in a scientific process that involves not only hard thinking but also trial and error. Don't be afraid to own your mistakes, to learn from them, and to keep moving forward.

17470884R00049

Made in the USA
Lexington, KY
11 September 2012